PEACE OF MIND AT AN EARLY AGE

PEACE OF MIND
AT AN EARLY AGE

by
Grace H. Pilon, SBS

Author of
THE WORKSHOP WAY®

VANTAGE PRESS
New York   Washington   Atlanta   Hollywood

TO
KATHARINE DREXEL, SBS
and the
YOUTH OF THE WORLD

CONTENTS

INTRODUCTION

INTRODUCTION

Many English words have more than one meaning. To be sure that the readers understand the *Formula for Peace of Mind* as presented in the following pages, the glossary is given here.

Affective Learning: is the learning that happens *while* learners *feel* important and *feel* intelligent.

Background: means the integrated factor, of heredity and environment. It is often considered the cause of success or failure in classrooms. *The Author of This Book Does Not Believe It.*

Becoming: is the process people live through that *begins at the moment a person uses initiative totally on one's own power* . . . and continues throughout one's life.

Behavior Change: is the happening that means a person *can never be the same again*. It is the moment of *change* towards greater amounts of "humanbeingness."

Cognitive Learning: is the learning of "things" that requires use of brain power; it exercises the "mind" for greater amounts of brain power in the future.

Creativity: is an *outcome*, a *fruit of healthy, human development*. It is a human skill that enables a person to handle his/her life, in a creative way, in order to accept the challenges—so-called "problems"—in ways that one can stay emotionally balanced, whatever happens day by day. Human beings express their creativity in many kinds of ways. Drawing, painting, creative writing are only a few ways. Unless children first grow towards *genuine creativity*, their painting, drawing, writing, and so forth—can be very superficial in the classroom.

Discovery: usually means the happening *in which people, big and little, become aware of their human powers, skills, and attitudes.* That happening is especially the time when people find out they can learn with their minds.

Discipline: is a power human beings have that can enable them to control their behavior. However, the power exists, at birth, but only as a seed that needs cultivation and nourishment. As human beings move towards full human development, they gain more and more mastery over this inner power.

Experiences: are those activities which often are left to the child to manage totally or arrange in his/her way. Personal experiences are opportunities for the child *to live his/her own life in order to learn how to live.*

Five Basic Dispositions: are the "seeds" of humanbeingness which every human being has at birth. They are love for truth (knowledge), sense of what is fair and just, acceptance of human existence with all its limitations, favorable attitudes towards work, and sense of cooperation (Maritain—1943).

Growth Points: are precise moments in the development of *persons* when people become more aware that they are human beings who can learn and think. The intensity of the awareness level determines the birth of new value systems in people (value—*feeling of one's worth only for being*). Value is not related at all to success or failure, to what one knows, or to mental abilities one has today!

Handling: is an opportunity a person has to become involved in activities in which one lives; it means that in the process of being involved "right answers" have equal value with "wrong answers." Right answers, or knowledge, is a by-product of the process.

Human Development: is the growth process in which human beings get to know about and to use human powers, human skills. It is the *growing into* humane attitudes towards self and others; it is the process of being lifted up for living on ever higher levels of consciousness.

Human Powers: are sense powers operating and are hopefully associated with intelligence by awareness of knowing or by "thinking" along with their use by persons. These powers are: seeing, hearing, listening, thinking, deciding, choosing, talking, and learning.

Human Skills: are initiative, independence in work habits, responsibility, courage, honesty, mutual respect, "risking," and *go-stop* power.

Human Attitudes (highly related to nourishment of five basic dispositions!): are outcomes of strong beliefs of human beings. For *peace of mind* these outcomes are essential: self-confidence, love of learning, joy over a job handled by beginning it—all in a logical order (from his/her value system), acceptance of human existence as it is with all its limitations, willingness to risk (to accept challenges of *"being alive"*), and willingness to cooperate in activities for growing and learning.

Inner Drive: is the characteristic unique in human beings that craves *"learning"* and *"thinking"* as nourishment for wanting to move and do things *just to be alive!*

Inner Order: is a *feeling of well being "in the mind."* It is an ability of consciousness, and to be sure of what one knows and sure of what one does not know. It is an ability that has to be nourished and developed, its presence nourishes emotional development.

Intellectual plane: is a phrase that names the nature of activities used to push human development. Activities demand the "handling of knowledge" by students *while they are in the act of learning* IT. The "handling" includes the right to risk answers, right or wrong, and the opportunities for decision making with teacher's use of WW* "cushioning" process operating so that, right or wrong, students believe they can live "learning" and still be *intelligent.*

Intellectual safety: is a phrase for naming a kind of human growth that gives people such a deep, strong feeling of worth as persons who can learn and think that they live in a state of mental security. It is the strongest human foundation that a person can have for *peace of mind.*

Learning Conditions: are factors in a person and out of a person that help human beings learn well academically. Example: Children are more apt to learn well in a pleasurable climate than in a hostile climate. There are many physical, social, mental, and emotional factors that help or hurt learning. Those factors that help learning are nourished by WW's philosophy and psychology.

Learning Styles: are the three kinds of personalities which WW calls strategies. Each kind of personality emerges when students have human characteristics in behavior that make their *time and way* of learning unique. WW has discovered that learning in groups of people with the same or nearly the same characteristics has power to make the interpersonal relationships within the group healthy and exciting.

WW from now on stands for: "Workshop Way® system of human development."

Since membership in any of the three groups does not depend upon knowledge or mental ability of today, changing from one group to another depends totally upon rate of human development. In each group the human being's basic needs for developing positive self-concepts are similar. Subject matter is handled in each group in the way needed to fit growth of human powers and skills.

Mental Development: is the process of lifting up people to higher levels of consciousness in *"being alive."* It's really just another name for the process of *becoming.*

Motivation: is the energy of the *inner drive.* If human beings do not like learning and thinking, they have much human development to get. It is the nature of humankind to like learning.

Outcomes: are skills, powers, and attitudes towards learning and growing that human beings get to possess at different times in their growth along the way.

Personal Business: means that children are people *now* and have a right to a time for growing. They do not want adults to talk to them or about them concerning their behavior, good or bad. Whatever adults do to lead children towards behavior in harmony with human dignity cannot be done in public and cannot be done "head on."

Principle of Individualization: This is a truth about human beings. All of them have different *ways* and different "time-clocks" within them for learning and growing. The way and the time do not determine who is "smart" and who is "not smart." The amount of knowledge one has often depends upon "accidents" of home, neighborhood, and schooling; knowledge is not a sign of more or less intelligence.

Problems: are only clues that tell teachers or parents what children need. Problems are essential to movements of growth in all living beings. Living implies CHANGE. Changes come about within the process of solving problems. Problems can be thought of as *"life hitting people in the face"* or *as opportunities for people to use their creativity in solving problems. Great things can happen by way of "problems."* *"You are not unusual, strange or sick if you have a problem!"* "Problems are not 'bad' things." Sorrow or joy can be part of problems. Sorrow is not "badness."

Retroactive Learning: is learning of which people become aware days, months, or years after the knowledge has been held in the subconscious. *"Intellectual safety"* has power to bring about this awareness.

Right Condition: is the author's term used for explaining her theory on behavior change and its relationship to *growing with learning academically.* Note, it is not being said that the relationship is to "right answers." A growth point with a deep intensity of awareness becomes "HOT" to the right degree to give birth to a new value system in a person . . . and *that point* is the *right condition for moving ahead in human development.*

Self-concept: is a feeling of some kind of worth as a person. A positive self-concept is a deep feeling of one's worth as a human being who can learn and think, *and nothing else in this world can interfere with that feeling.* A negative self-concept is a deep feeling of one's nothingness in this world. It exists and can be effected by other forces, because self-concept develops along a line or continuum of many points. When you reach the far right end, that's it; it's as far as a person can go. If you are on any other point, you have a right and ability to move up to any point beyond yours.

Strategies: —are sometimes people with like personalities;
—are sometimes procedures to fit the needs for the different groups of like personalities;

—are discovered ways of individualizing "learning to learn" and "learning to think" within whole groups of students for teaching and learning.

Chapter ten explains the strategies.

Testing Atmosphere: is a climate in which children are forced to grow day after day *being perfect already* in the eyes of the adults at home or in school. When signs of imperfection show up in behavior or learning patterns, children are made to suffer humiliation through punishment, or ridicule, often even by being called "stupid." It is also an environment in which teachers mark everything children do and awareness of their weaknesses goes deeper into their minds and hearts rather than awareness of their strengths.

Values: are deep, strong convictions people have of their worth as human beings, who can learn, think, and handle their lives. Values are powerful determiners of human behavior in that they influence a person's choices in all areas of life. They can lead people to mutual respect or to bitterness and hatred of people and authority. Values along with the operation of the *principle of individualization* can insure that mutual respect be present in any kind of group.

Chapter One

HUMAN POWERS, SKILLS, AND ATTITUDES

A kindergarten child is on the floor working a *"thinker."* Kim has a white card with "1" on it and another white card with "2" on it. She has 20 pink cards. All of the pink cards have either one or two objects printed on them. Kim's job is to make a decision for every card about where to place the pictures—under the "1" or under the "2." The child is allowed to figure out the *way* by herself. A visitor approaches, looks at the work and says, "My, but you're smart!" Kim looks up at the adult without any show of being overwhelmed by the compliment and says, "Everybody's smart in this room!"

Another day a first grader walked by Jane's desk, looked at her work and informed her that the work was all wrong. Jane's reply without anger or unhappiness was, *"Well*! My brain does not have to work like your brain!" Jane paid him no more attention and continued with what she was doing. The self-appointed okayer walked away, knowing Jane was right about their differences.

In order to learn well academically and to maintain emotional health in the process of living ten years in the classrooms of the United States, children need nourishment and development of human skills, powers, and convictions of worth *early in their educational growth*. Here is a list of the essential needs:

Human Powers:

sharpened abilities to see and to hear *intelligently*
learning how to learn
learning how to think
listening
talking

Human Skills:

initiative;
independence in work habits;
courage to risk, regardless of consequences, in order to learn;
honesty in facing what I know and what I don't know;
honesty in seeking help whenever I need it;
courage it takes to live according to the *principle of individualization;*
ability to make decisions and to accept consequences;
responsibility to handle one's life and whatever it calls for in the process! and
go-stop power (ability to control starting and stopping of acitivities).

Attitudes and Convictions:

positive self-concept;
love of learning;
feeling joy over a job performed, knowing well "I" handled this—beginning it, moving on towards the finish line, and finally ended it—knowing "I" did it!
acceptance of human existence as it is with all its limitations;
willingness to cooperate in the activities for learning and growing;
a strong sensing of what is fair and just kept healthy, safeguarded in a just and fair "adult-child" environment" of close human relationships; and
willingness to admit mistakes along the way because "I" will find a way to handle them.

How are these powers, skills and attitudes nourished? Chil-

2

dren follow a "Workshop Schedule" of tasks all day whenever they are not with teachers. Children assume the responsibility to do these tasks according to *their understanding of them.* The *five freedoms* of the program are operating; *these freedoms create the peer interpersonal relationships*—and become the *opportunities* for children to *handle* their own personality "clashes," if any, and to assist each other with the good and the less good happenings.

This kind of practice (handling one's life) for living in the real world is essential for children to learn how to live humanely. *Teachers* teach all day and "in between teaching groups" there are ways to bring about healthy teacher-child relationships. The following pages of this chapter discuss other ways of nourishing human abilities in the classroom. Parents can adapt the ideas to continue the healthy human development in the home.

Children must become convinced that everyone is different, so they do not need to worry about where others are in the schedule. They relax as they work. Workshop Way children are sure that "timing" is not related to intelligence. They live according to their beliefs. Remember the child in kindergarten who told the visitor—"Everyone is smart in here."

Throughout the day children know when the individual, or group, or whole class lessons happen.

Knowing what comes next throughout the day keeps the students feeling non-threatened.

A large schedule is put up in the room that tells what the teachers are doing and what the children are doing.

Effective learning and healthy growing depend upon the consistency of the teachers to do whatever is done in the framework of WW philosophy and psychology.

Whatever has been said about the climate, order, and interpersonal relationships in the classrooms can be used by parents to create a growing climate at home to insure that children can be psychologically and emotionally safe while learning.

Children, regardless of age, need to learn that mistakes and any other kind of "failure" are steps towards making the brains

3

healthy because even the mistakes and failures can force movement in the brain cells and prevent brains from getting "rusty" or frozen. Exercising the brain cells pushes children towards creativity and language living. Teachers talk to children about the brain in ways that relate to each level of learners. It is very important children understand this language.

It is not enough to have creativity. People need human powers and skills to be brave enough to live their creativity. That takes courage, initiative, fearlessness in risking independent work, fearlessness in making mistakes, and *willingness to share bursts of excitement for what is happening—all this without fear of being "laughed at."*

What good is creativity if the owner is afraid to use it?

As individuals gain in human skills and powers, they *feel important*; self-confidence begins to flower.

Handling one's life in doing the tasks also helps children to gain these skills. Praising human powers nourishes courage in using the powers without fear. Teaching sessions provide more nourishment for willingness to cooperate and to participate.

Teachers shock the brain cells of their students daily by the way they relate *all content* to human thought and offer opportunities for risking the knowledge skills even before children have the knowledge fully.

WW deliberately wants and plans for ALL CHILDREN to have wrong answers sometimes so they can learn to cope with them without losing emotional balance.

Grouping children according to their personality traits is one way to polish human powers and skills. It enables existence of group teaching effectively. You will learn more about the strategies in Chapter Ten.

NOTE: *Children know that knowledge and intelligence are not the criteria for belonging to any certain group.* There's Louie in the Strategy C Group; he knows everything! Helen can really think; yet she is a Strategy C Learner! Tom can't sit still and he is a Strategy C Learner! Respect for peers and timing in doing and reacting to teacher directions have much to do with grouping. I should add "respect for self" is a factor in placement.

Strategy learners are only taught with strategy procedures in the major subject matter lessons. All the rest of the day children work alone, or with groups of their choosing, doing the tasks in the workshop. Example, a "Strategy C Learner" is not a "Strategy C Learner" all day. He/she may even be a genius. However, this discovery might never be made unless the system of education deliberately planned the work and curriculum in a way that children are free to reveal themselves accurately. A work-life environment in which children handle the work *their way* provides teachers and parents with information every day. Parents are free to be in WW classrooms as much as they want—to visit, to sit by their children, or to share their talents. Every day the adults can know where students are right now in human development and by the same means supply them knowledge at the time when the students change behavior to meet the need for more difficult challenges and to move students up to higher levels of living consciously. The new change is usually accompanied with greater ability to use human power for acquiring human skills and positive attitudes about life in general.

Gradually *peace of mind* will become part of the total person.

The greatest factor in leading children towards *peace of mind* and the use of human faculties is *consistency* in adult behavior *at every movement of growth along the way, the adults respect* the *now* products, behavior, and learning patterns of the children.

Chapter Two

KNOWING IS NOT GROWING

Knowledge is the by-product of the process. It is the process that moves growing.

Knowledge can belong to people with fantastic memories. When it comes to people this way, it is usually easy to recall and it can give joy—but no iota of it has power to change human behavior "upwards." It can change human behavior "downwards." I have known, and my readers surely have known, people with much knowledge and little common sense or respect for other people. The very knowledge they have can cause some people to think they are superior to others. It can cause them to look upon people with less learning as inferior and worthy of cold treatment. The *principle of individualization* is not operating for these people.

Note: *many people can get their knowledge because of powerful memories* and be people who care about themselves and others. Their *human growth* does not depend upon their knowledge. It comes to them by accident, because people in their homes or school allow them the freedom to be themselves in the events of each day. Handling the "content" that faces them daily supplies the process which they can handle since they already have much human growth to begin with.

Knowledge can come to people because they unconsciously

6

participate in activities supplied by good parents and teachers. Workshop Way® does not depend upon past environments of children for the teachers to believe that *all children can learn;* but WW does not deny that some children come to school with knowledge that peers do not have because of their rich social and educational backgrounds.

When knowledge is not the by-product of the *process* discussed in this book, the persons concerned often depend upon their knowledge as the substance of their life and happiness. Let a little failure, even one instance of humiliation because of not knowing one "something," and the students become emotionally overwhelmed and frustrated. When knowledge is the by-product of the process, children can face failure or success and continue *to feel their own worth* because they are dead-sure *their value or worth does not come from knowledge.* A person's human value system makes a difference! *Peace of mind* cannot be an on-going experience for people who think they are worth what they know or worth what they have.

> Children are almost totally dependent upon teachers and parents for the kind of value system they develop along the way of growing and learning each day!

What is meant by process? Let me use the "teaching-learning of reading" concept as the way to explain process. Everyone cannot learn how to read well if a method is used to try to do it. Everyone can learn how to read well if the way to success is a process.

> As long as knowledge skills have first priority in a system of instruction, process is impossible. Why? Because the pressure put upon people to learn anything with perfection automatically brings fear into the picture. Fear freezes the brain power of many students. If people directing perfection of knowledge skills *would not demand the perfection even while children are supposed to be learning them,* the emotional damage would not be so great. When a school system's idea of excellence is in the area of knowledge skills,

pressure is placed upon adults—teachers in classrooms and parents at home. The tension passes from adults into students.

The process consists of the *personal experiences* that students live through while handling the subject matter—reading in this case. The word that makes a difference between process and method is "live." Living requires willingness to be involved, regardless of consequences of right or wrong answers. *This kind of cooperation is only possible in groups wherein every child feels important and intellectually safe. Therefore, priority has to be given to development of positive self-concepts!* For example, one of the first skills children need to acquire in order to read is *courage.* So courage is applauded in order to develop in students the value that courage is more important *than a right answer.* After all we only need to know a "right answer" when a one-time situation calls for it. *But courage!!?? Now that's something we need all our lives if* we want to keep on living, learning, and being happy.

The *process* would cease being if we applauded right answers. All students cannot be expected to get the right answers at the same time, even in the same year. If right answers are applauded, the act allows children to believe they have worth if they know something well and that they have little worth if they do not know something well now. As a result some children get false values for living; other children become depressed with the feelings of their nothingness and inferiority within the group.

On the other hand if wrong answers and right answers are understood to have equal value *while knowledge is being learned,* students can enjoy risking oral and written answers in activities (living) since they are *dead-sure their worth does not depend upon either kind of answer.*

Here the foundation is being laid for genuine *peace of mind* while growing and learning.

Process includes awareness and feelings in children of the joy of "*being alive.*" The process for learning how to read includes a sequence of uninterrupted reading activities throughout a whole day. Even children who think they can't read *must read if it takes teachers to "Lend their brains" to them for their first reading experiences!*

Example: Teacher shows word, "come." She/he says, "You know this says come, don't you?" Teacher waits for a response to her/his "don't you?" Then, "Let's count the letters in this word" (can't be worried about the knowledge skill: "recognition of letter names"). *Children can count.* Build upon what children know.

Teacher points to each letter. Children count each letter. "*What did we just count?*" (Note: teacher is pushing for living language experiences.)

Teacher adds two choices for answers after she asks the question: "apples or letters?"

"Beautiful! You know what letters are. Words are made out of letters. Right?" (Teacher waits for response to "right?")

Teacher: "What's right? Encourage volunteers to answer their way. Every response is right in that it took courage to volunteer it. Applaud the courage. Teacher tells right answer if volunteer says something that is not true.

Teacher points to word "come." "Is this word—pie or come?" (*Wait for response.*)

Adults always wait for response whenever they ask something. WHY? If they don't, children unconsciously get idea that adults do not think they have anything important to say!

Concrete respect demands that adults wait.

Teacher shows flash card with "come" on it. Children get books! "Let's look at the first page. Find all the *comes* you can find. Read each *come* and touch it before finding others."

Occasionally teacher asks, "what are you doing?" The answer must be "reading."

Children find *comes* on other pages.

The lesson goes on in this manner—getting children involved in doing and saying—listening and applauding—*living* in the *process.* In this way children who think they can't read *begin to feel important,* having lived through personal experiences which had meaning and even success. As soon as a child begins to take the initiative in the activities, at that moment *the child begins his/her process of becoming.* Getting chilren *to say what they are doing* is necessary to lead them to the awareness of *being alive!* This awareness and *feeling of success* nourishes inner drive which should be motivation enough for any human being to want to learn and to live. When education consists of process, it yields *outcomes*—natural powers of human beings. These powers are listed below.

KNOWLEDGE
CREATIVITY
SHARPENED SENSE AND PERCEPTUAL SKILLS
MUTUAL RESPECT IN A GROUP
POSITIVE SELF-CONCEPTS

Peace of mind formula demands that the process be directed by adults who safeguard children in it so they always maintain human dignity and respect. There could be *what looks like process* in innovated kinds of education but it can't be process in its essence if the priority value is still on the knowledge skills and especially *if artificial kinds of motivation are used to keep the children* looking busy and enjoying the activities. If adults continue to drill the knowledge skills without creating living language opportunities, special relationships between teachers and students that can make children feel their worth will not happen.

If "the children love it" is the factor that determines the teacher's procedure for creating activity, the activity is not *process.* Naturally children love knowledge they have and can show that they have it. For *human growth, teacher/parent artistry* in moving it requires *that children live in the activities with willingness to be involved without having to fear* or to worry about the knowledge skills *at this minute.* Dynamic activities require opportunities for *risking* and *making decisions* with willingness to accept the consequences. Any praise of knowledge skills would take away the "dynamic" nature of the involvement.

In the process of teaching reading, children must do all the reading, all of the time, in their lesson sessions. "I can read" is an awareness all students need if they are to grow towards positive self-concepts and peace of mind. *This is why school systems that give first priority to child development and not to knowledge skills* cannot allow teachers and a few students in a group to use up the time "discussing the story" in order that children will learn values from the story. Children grow values from the inside. Stories and/or adult example cannot *give* children values. We know this is true just by thinking of any family. Children have the same example always before them; but children in the same family do not have the same value systems from which they behave.

Individualization of subject matter does not meet human being basic needs *if every child in our schools is to learn well* and to maintain emotional health throughout ten years or more. Consideration of the child as a human person must have priority. The author lists these human being basic needs. If needs are satisfied in the learning process of school systems, children can live at peace.

> *intellectual safety*
> *inner order*
> *feeling of one's ability to create and to organize*
> *doing satisfying work on one's own time* and not in competition with peers
> feeling of ease in relating to people, peers or adults
> a healthy sense of cooperation

Students *need individualization* in the development of human powers, skills, and a growing towards positive attitudes of living itself.

This kind of process can only happen in classrooms where individualization of human living is allowed. It is the only way teachers can discover a person's needs in human powers. Then the use of content in process can satisfy these needs. Learning that comes through process releases greater brain power. Citizens of a democracy need highly developed intelligence in order to handle freedoms with common sense and mutual respect.

11

Chapter Three

DISCIPLINE

Discipline is a power human beings have that can enable them to control their behavior. Unhappily people are not born with it. The power is there at birth as a seed that requires nourishment and development. The seed is nourished: 1) by a sense of inner order; 2) by development of the five basic dispositions children have by nature; and 3) by an awareness that one has this power and the courage to use it in the art of living.

Hence, educational systems must begin to develop inner order as soon as children enter our schools. This is why the five basic dispositions are always being nourished if the Workshop Way content is used in schools with priority being given to development of the person. This is why the system of human development for education called Workshop Way® is constantly lifting up children to higher levels of consciousness.

Nourishment of inner order consists of:

1) Adults at home and in school make sure there is plenty of outer order in the environment without pressure on child. The author believes that vivid outer order projects order into a person's mind and feeds inner order proper nourishment. This is only one way to help.

2) Confusion in the mind has to go. How?

a) Children know with certainty who they are. They *FEEL*

they have worth because of the way adults treat them at all times.

b) Children develop an honesty about their knowledge. The feeling of "I have worth because of what I know" has to go! A technique used in WW frequently is that of getting children to say with power what they know and *to say with power*, "I don't know that!"

c) Children require opportunities to say and to feel "what they know now"; but they also need to be convinced that what they don't know can be always learned now or later.

That is not enough. Children must be dead-sure that the time when they learn anything does not make them "smart" or "not smart."

d) Adults help to bring children alive to know where they are now, to know what they are doing now, and to affirm this "knowing" within them by having children say occasionally *what is happening now.*

3) Children undergo a process in which they will get to know and to feel that they are intellectually safe. This particular process means that adults constantly "cushion" them to become dead-sure that they are human beings with human powers; but, that these powers take time to grow. While they are making mistakes in behavior and in learning, it is vital that children *feel they hold on to their intelligence.* It is not enough for children to know this truth about themselves; they must be helped to believe the truth is for their peers, too.

At any moment any of us will be the victim of our own mistakes or of the mistakes of others. The mistakes are not what we should worry about.

It is how we handle the consequences of the mistakes that makes the difference.

WHO makes the mistake is not important knowledge!

Here again we see the application of WW's individualization. Each person is a world unto himself/herself. Both adults and peers need to recognize this in order to keep them from judging everyone alike. The needs of one are not the needs of the other outside of the human being's basic needs as listed by WW's philosophy. Human beings may all be different; but, *they all have something exactly the same! human nature*

Perhaps this is the place to point out the dangers of so-called traditional ideas in regard to discipline. To the traditionalist, what looks like discipline is not discipline. What actually is happening is that children are taking on forced behavior patterns. They cannot be themselves; therefore, growth is stunted. Whatever the adults believe to be discipline will determine a healthy or an unhealthy environment for child development. If the traditionalists get their way, then children will be punished or publicly humiliated because of *"things"* while their *persons* go underdeveloped or rather—developed in a negative way which breeds hatred and bitterness for people and the world at large!

Rigid disciplinary policies put all students in the same mold. Children are taught and even forced to behave one way to be "good." When the students leave the system, unless home influence makes a difference, they have to face unique worlds requiring different kinds of handling; but they only learned one way. Sit straight; move quietly; above all do not talk or chew gum; and don't come late to school! Do everything I tell you to do and we will get along just fine!

> If children are forced to behave this one way throughout ten years of their lives, why should adults be surprised if so many young people need to go out of themselves to find a *feeling of importance*?

Often the kinds of behavior wanted are what teachers and parents want for their own satisfaction. They want other adults to look at them (parents and teachers) as "good" disciplinarians. They feel proud of their abilities to discipline children. *What about the children?*

Parents and educators, beware of quiet classrooms, of quiet younsters! Consider some of the things that the quiet and rigid classrooms do to too many children. Barring those children whose home environment is psychologically and emotionally so healthy that it prevents negative happenings from effecting children permanently, the rigid classroom without movement or talking tends:

To fill children with fear that freezes the brain cells and prevents many children from learning and many other children from learning as well as they could.

To fill children with distrust of adults in society.

To engender hatred of authority.

To engender hatred of school.

To fire up an unhealthy kind of competition in which only winners have human worth.

To prevent development of positive self-concepts children need to make them feel their worth as persons who can learn and think.

To compel children to seek excitement secretly which can build up in them guilt feelings.

To make children vulnerable intellectually because the only values they are aware of are quietness and good marks.

NOTE: The author does not deny that these negative outcomes can also be present in nontraditional classes if teachers and parents hold on to the traditional values about behavior in school in the name of discipline.

As long as knowledge skills remain the sign of personal success there is little chance for nourishment of the five basic dispositions. If children receive this nourishment in their homes, they can survive the inhuman policies in classrooms in the name of discipline. If not, then the children, the families, and the country must suffer the consequences in the type of citizens who will be living in a democracy. *For these children schools have to take on the family spirit;* children need a place where they can do their own living in order to learn how to live. They need *personal experiences that they handle* in order to become aware that they are *alive.* Children must have exercise in creating their own kind of order while they are growing. This kind of growing requires adults to accept the products of the students regardless of how they look to the adults. Acceptance means adults give concrete respect to what they look like and are doing today!

Much talking is essential among the students who are doing the learning and the growing. The climate calls for adults who can stand or who are willing to learn how to stand certain amounts of noise and movement. If learning is to be exciting to children, they must not be afraid to move and to talk *on their own initiative*.

Learning cannot be exciting to *all* children if it takes motivation that exists outside of persons to make it interesting. Artificial motivation is not only unnecessary for human beings, but often a waste of time for some students. It is during that time that the students can get turned off on learning and they begin to create excitement not related to the subject at hand.

Human beings, by nature, should be interested in learning "Whatever" is up for learning.

If they are not, their natural source of motivation—inner drive—must be dried up.

Real learning experiences, wherein right and wrong answers have equal value, are able to captivate the learners, nourish inner drive, and get rid of the competition factor that determines only a few can ever be the winners.

Why don't many children like school? The author ventures the following reasons:

The children do not have peace of mind because they must live five to six hours a day in the "rat race" of good marks for learning knowledge skills; that's all school means to them.

There is probably no special relationship between the teacher and the learners of the content. When that is missing children become aware that things are more important to people in that atmosphere. When right answers become the only value teachers know, they have power to make students feel stupid or smart according to what they know *today*. So many children give up hope.

Why? They can't bear living in a testing atmosphere all day, every day. Students *feel* teachers do or do not like them because of their inability to learn everything fast enough to suit the teachers. Students *feel* this rejection—real or imaginary.

If discipline is valued by teachers more than the content, children feel rejection when the teacher's eyes frequently meet theirs as "force prods" to get them to listen and to work. Children are bound to believe they are not being trusted because of the killing looks of the adults.

Artificial motivation delays the development of initiative and independence in work habits. Artificial motivation is not strong enough to inspire children who know their teachers and parents are only satisfied with perfection in the work they do. No time is allowed for children to grow towards perfection. Children are *born with a sense of what is fair and just.* Because of their very own nature, they are forced to react negatively to demands of adults that are unjust. Children *have a right to grow* which means they *have a right to produce inferior products along the way.* Their greatest achievement during the time of growing is to be willing to live in the presence of adults.

TRUE VALUES which put worth on persons rather than upon things allow adults to *respect different degrees of quality in work products and in human behavior while students are learning and growing.* **Safeguards for preservation of human dignity and feelings of self-worth in students:**

A policy of applauding human powers and skills must exist. This policy demands that knowledge skills are never applauded.

People are not applauded for walking. Learning is what people are supposed to be doing.

Knowledge skills are by-products of the growth process.
Too much praise of human powers can become disgusting to

children. Adults observe and learn the right amounts of praise that their children can handle well.

Self-discipline is the goal of school systems wherein persons are more valuable than things.

Chapter Four

HOPE FOR THE FUTURE

An administrator in education once asked the author, "How is it that you can reach children that no one else seems to be able to reach?"

I hope this question is answered by the time the reader finishes this book.

If the ultimate goal of education is full human development *for all children to their greatest potential*, then the means to that end must be feasible or it should not contain words—for *all children*.

Workshop Way® is a system of human development for education and its goal is to make the means to that end feasible for *all* children by *lifting them up to higher levels of conscious living so that 100% of our students can learn academically in school*. This "lifting up" process can be done by developing human powers, human skills, and positive attitudes in children towards growing and learning. This process *must come first before knowledge skills are demanded from all students at the same time if all are to see success*.

When content (subject matter) is used to nourish human powers as a first priority in our classrooms and knowledge skills given second priority in foundational grades, then children are *freed from fear* and they can grow and learn with happiness.

Emotional development goes hand in hand with mental development.

The philosophy of this new system of human development for education requires all adults involved in the learning and growing process to believe: 1) *That children are people now and so deserve respect and reverence as such; 2) that all children can learn much better* than they are doing now; and 3) *that all children must have time to grow.* This latter belief calls for adults to look upon the mistakes of children during the process as necessary parts of the whole learning process; therefore, mistakes are to be expected and the children are not humiliated for them.

One can make a mistake and still feel intelligent!

The psychology of the WW system safeguards human dignity in the process of learning subject matter. If the principles are followed, children develop *within them* a condition of *"intellectual safety."* "Intellectual safety" is a mental security that allows persons to live *feeling safe* from any kind of a threat. It is a condition that allows children to enjoy success in school.

The teacher is the facilitator of growth in classrooms and parents direct the growth in their homes. Both teachers and parents need to know the philosophy and psychology of the WW. In WW "learning style" is a phrase used that means a child's present ability to use brain power and a child's present personality traits.

The "learning styles" of individuals are *not permanent states.* If people are continuously enjoying human development, their "learning styles" are constantly changing whenever the people begin to live at a higher level of awareness of *being alive with human skills.* This happens because people discover that they are persons who can learn and think at ever deeper awareness levels. *Each movement of awareness helps human beings to know they are living with power to control their lives.*

When children go to school, some of them can learn now and some of them cannot learn now, *right?*

I do not believe this! No one knows how much learning power anyone has.

It is thought that the fact of heredity and the reality of different kinds of socio-economic and ethnic groups as experience backgrounds make it necessary for school systems to use different approaches to learning to fit the so-called backgrounds. A common approach to that problem is that of finding ways to develop other kinds of abilities that these children might have.

I do not believe this is good enough for human beings!

I believe *all* human beings require an awareness of intellectual ability to have a permanent, positive self-concept so they can be happy, productive human beings and healthy citizens of their society.

People have individual differences—true. Also, true, is that all people have the same human nature!

This belief is what gives WW its power to reach everyone. WW's entire system of *human development for education* has built in safeguards to prevent hurting human nature; the system nourishes what is "good" in human nature in order to bring out what is *best in each person.*

When children must live with undeveloped human faculties because some people judge them as inadequate learners of academic studies, and if *testing to find out weaknesses and strengths in students* takes place before the undeveloped human faculties have been nourished in ways that do not depend upon knowledge skills, *then* educators and psychologists will find out learning disabilities by examining the test results.

WW's position is that all children have a right to have their five basic dispositions nourished before their lives depend upon test results.

WW believes in giving tests to inform coordinators of curriculum if the quality of instruction is good enough to give students power sufficient to produce continuous progress in all subject matter areas.

If not, it is up to the administration to change the quality of instruction for learning to learn and learning to think!

WW also believes in testing to nourish enthusiasm in teachers. If the quality of instruction is suitable for growth of human powers, human skills, and positive attitudes in students towards learning and growing, the test results will show continuous progress in all subject matter areas.

Systems of education that depend upon a grade level equivalent to evaluate the quality of teacher or pupil performance *have missed the point of the concept of individualization in child development.*

When children must live with adults who treat them as if they are not human yet, children cannot show behavior in harmony with human dignity. Both parents and teachers need to adopt consistent behavior in their relationships between themselves and their children. In order to nourish inner drive, *it takes the consistent behavior of adults.* It is very important *to impress children at every opportunity with what they can do and say while they are growing and learning.*

Whatever children do, say, and or produce *while they are learning requires respect* from adults in the environment at home or in school. When the adults see behavior or products they do not like, the adults must learn how to teach and re-teach instead of constantly correcting or punishing.

Adults value "the *knowing* of subject matter" highly; often children do not have this value, except for the reward received or for the punishment and shame avoided. *NOTE, however,* that the reward or the punishment has no power to get children to do what they should do, by nature, *love learning.*

I do not believe it has to be this way. Learning disabilities

22

and emotionally disturbed behavior are highly related to the existence or nonexistence of development of the five basic dispositions that children, by nature, have, namely;

> *a love of truth* (knowledge)
> *a sense of what is fair and just*
> *acceptance of limitations of human existence*
> *a sense of well-being in the doing and finishing of work*
> *a sense of cooperation*[1]

Child-centered classrooms are fertile places where these dispositions get rich nourishment. Here children handle their own "doings" throughout the day by following a "Workshop Schedule," a *thing*—that cannot hurt people.

When children finish jobs with an awareness of what they are doing, and with security in knowing what comes next in the doing of the jobs, and finally with a feeling of satisfaction in knowing the job is done, they feel joy and they *feel important*.

Why?

The order of the activities satisfies a child's need for *feeling order* in the process of doing something—and the need for *feeling important* in the independent handling of the job.

> Awareness of knowing one has power to do things on one's own brings with it—joy and *peace of mind.*

> The beginning, middle, end concept is *basic to the order the "brain" craves and basic to the development of self-discipline!*

In WW, the process of lifting up people to live on higher levels of consciousness, consists of *daily, personal experiences* wherein persons risk handling situations regardless of the consequences

---

1. Maritain, Jacques, *Education at the Crossroads* (New Haven: Yale University Press, 1943), pp. 36-38 (ahead of his time with educational ideas that most authors of today, who are humanists, are writing about and talking about).

and regardless of their present state of knowledge skills. During *all activities in workshop and in teaching sessions, wrong and right answers have equal value.*

Parents and all other educators must begin to allow students to make mistakes while learning and to be able to *feel intelligent while doing so!*

When that right of learners becomes more widespread in our country, then our children will be able to:

see better;
hear better;
think better;
and learn better.

Healthy human development cannot be equated with development of knowledge skills.

Knowledge should be the by-product of the process of education.

If it is not, it should be.

When knowledge skills have first priority, all children cannot be reached for learning in school.

Important! If all children in the United States of America must live ten years in classrooms, they must be reached early . . . even in the kindergarten . . . or better yet in their homes . . . to give them power to learn how to learn and to learn how to think. Workshop Way® is one way to do this. Its system allows freedom to students to be actively involved in their own process of growing and learning *all day long, every day.* WW has been used at every level of learning from pre-school to universities.

It has been the experience of teachers involved in the programs for ten years that if the philosophy and psychology of the system are followed, learning disabilities are either lessened or removed. When a school system insists that *all* students receive *equal reverence and respect* wherever they are in the learning and growing process, *all students can move towards a positive self-concept with ever-deepening awareness of their worth* as persons who can learn and think.

If students sense that they are "valued" at home and in school because they learn, think, and act on an adult time table determined by a testing atmosphere, they will fear, distrust and hate authority. The strain of having to always have the right answer, little by little, drains a person's *inner drive* for living humanely and happily.

If parents and teachers tell children every move to make at home and in schools, there is no time or place for children to *begin to be.*

> *Beginning to be requires a first time movement on part of child that is entirely initiated by him/her and executed by the child while he/she is relaxed mentally–free from fear.*
>
> *The child becomes aware of the power he/she has in managing self.* Now there is more than *being! There is living!* This *experience in being alive is personal success. This kind of personal success is rich nourishment for development of the five basic dispositions and of positive self-concepts.*

Here is my idea of how human growth moves towards its fullness. Let the entire growth period be represented by a line:

(animal-like   (behavior in harmony
behavior)   ·····✳···········✳···   with human dignity—
                                         full human development)

Let the dots represent millions of growth points that happen within the total growth process.)

There are also many invisible "growth points"; but some points become *special ones* which are reached at a time when the person is enjoying a new awareness depth of self as a person who can learn and think. That's the "right condition" for a new value system to be born in the person. Then he/she can never be the same again.

For example, a child in a third-grade classroom had the habit of upsetting the classroom daily. He showed anger and bitterness and no love for working as his usual behavior. One day he was involved with a game called a *"thinker."* The teacher gave the lunch time signal to put everything away. Our boy became very angry and vented his wrath upon the teacher: "I hate you! I hate you! I hate you!" *Then, suddenly, something happened for the first time.*

> The boy's face softened and his voice came through with great sincerity, "Oh! No, I don't! No, I don't. No, I don't."

> It was a tremendous experience for everyone. Teacher and children were deeply happy about what they were seeing and feeling!

The child's behavior reflected his NEW GROWTH POINT and a change in the child's behavior. All of WW's policies and uses of procedures and materials exist to nourish deliberately whatever a student needs in any *now time* of the school year for movement of human development. The author believes and has evidence over a period of many years to justify the belief that any human weakness in learning and in social behavior can be treated effectively by moving human growth through intense mental involvement in daily activities, with persons *feeling important and intelligent in the process.* One cannot "de-grow!"

> The farther the "growth point" moves towards the right, human traits appear that were never discernable before, and one's behavior becomes more and more in harmony with human dignity. (*Process of becoming*)

If children take psychological tests or other kinds of tests while there "growth points" are towards the left side of the line, the pseudo-learning disabilities will be identified. *Planned human development makes sure that perceptual skills are highly related to human intelligence.* WW plans human development at a high degree of probability. It is *not left to chance.* The stronger the relationship between the senses and the intelligence, the sharper the senses become. WW's tasks in the work-life atmosphere and WW's *psychology of teaching merged with philosophy for living in learning climates* supply the sense-intelligence related experiences all day, every day.

Content is for children and not children for content. Students must handle the content of their grade level of learning regardless of right-wrong answers in the process. *All children,* regardless of what adults think or of what tests indicate about their abilities of the moment, *must have equal opportunities in the handling of the grade-level content in some way.* WW has three distinct and very specific ways in allowing children with different personalities to handle *all the grade level content.* (See Chapter Ten.)

Remember this: No one knows anyone's potential—ever!

All children need is to be allowed to live a way of life filled with personal experiences in the *management of self-directed activities* with *adults in their environment respecting concretely whatever quality of products* children produce on their own power *along the way* of growing and learning, day by day.

In the United States all children are forced, by law, to live, at least, ten years of their lives in classrooms. *Implications:*

    1. Every child has a right to the power needed for academic success.

    2. Society has the responsibility to see that every child *gets that power.*

Is it feasible to give every child power to learn in school? *Yes. It is happening today in classrooms across the country* where parents and educators are brave enough to allow development of human powers *first*.

It is happening today in many homes where children create their own workshops for "playing" after school.

In Coldwater, Michigan, a seventh grader created a fantastic workshop in her basement. It is designed to interest age levels from first through seventh grades. Friends and neighbors in this *teenager's* block spend one to two hours after school enjoying the tasks the seventh grader *created*.

WW is a flexible framework for easy adaptation at all levels of learning *and for any programs a school might have*.

WW does not depend upon a system's curriculum. *It does depend upon WW's formula in the use of time, philosophy, and psychology*.

By word of mouth of teachers and lately, of children, WW materials and *way* of operating have reached all fifty states of the U.S.A. and into a few foreign countries.

Xavier University of New Orleans sponsors the Workshop Way® Program. It concentrates on in-service courses, workshops, and/or institutes, every summer.

At WW's Second Annual Convention in New York City at Manhattan College in 1977, an association was formed, called The National Association for Workshop Way® Educators. The word "educators" was chosen instead of "teachers" because it is hoped that *parents will become members and show their power towards change in education that brings equal opportunities for learning and growing to all children and that these opportunities will not depend upon what adults think about the abilities of their children nor upon what testing evidence says about their children*.

Be sure to note that WW does believe in a certain amount of testing to nourish *enthusiasm in teachers* and *parents* for the growing and learning that can happen *to their students*.

Chapter Five

WHAT ARE "PROBLEMS"???

Problems are those experiences in our lives—which can be painful and which can, also, make us ieel that we have failed in some way. However, it takes "problems" to challenge our use of human power and creativity as we move along in human growth. Now human beings are not born with the fullness of creativity. Although the seed of creativity is possessed at birth, it must be nourished. *Creativity is the outcome of the process of human development* and it will suddenly overflow in one's life, *if the five basic dispositons are healthily nourished and developed.*

What good is creativity if persons haven't the courage, initiative, self-confidence, and responsibility to handle it and to follow through on the callings of inspiration that come at some time or other to all human beings.

Splashing paint around, making up rhymes in poetry, and creating stories are superficial signs of creativity in people who were allowed to handle paint, poetry, and prose in original ways. Genuine creativity is *the handling of life by human beings who enjoy security in their own "people worlds."*

The development of talent is something different. The author believes if children are free *to live while learning*, they'll get the basics in subject matter during the first four or five years of elementary education. She recommends as a *major change* in education that the last four or five years of elementary education be fully given the study by personal interests all day, every day, or fully given to the development of individual talents all day, every day.

There is a WW school now, in 1977, in New Orleans where two-thirds or more of the students *are now ready for this new change in education.* Unhappily it takes specially equipped classrooms for intensive study in subjects of special interest to students: such as—math, science, literature, drama, music, art, dance, gymnastics, and others. It takes specially prepared teachers in each of these areas to be hired on a fulltime basis.

The author's dream is that these specialists would start their day in the early afternoon. Children now achieving success in the basics could spend every afternoon in the area of their choice. Children who need more years of study in the basics could share the enrichment by attending classes of their choices after the school day is over. Sometimes dreams come true. *What a country would we have in the United States of America*!!

Can you imagine what it would be like in high schools if the students enrolled were grounded in the basics and prepared to specialize in the subjects of their interests!

As parents and teachers along with administrators learn more about a system of human development for education, the two-thirds figure would increase.

Why and when did the word-problem-come to be considered something like a bad monster in our lives?

I don't know; but I do know that wherever there is life that is healthy *there will be problems.* Life means change. Change always holds out problems to be solved.

PROBLEMS IN SCHOOL

Problems are "clues" that tell teachers when it is time to move students either in the way they are learning or in the way they are behaving. In either case, the same therapy works: challenging students to come alive by being willing to use human faculties in risking in order to learn how to learn and to learn how to think.

In order to sustain the health of the *inner drive* of individuals who along the way of growing require more difficult curricular development, teachers and parents must be able to give these children new challenges to meet new needs. This responsibility of adults demands that *first of all* they must know the children as well as they possibly can. WW deliberately sets up an environment that allows children to reveal themselves accurately in both human skills and in knowledge skills. One example of how the system does this is as follows:

From grades 1 through 8, the first half hour is used to allow children complete freedom to begin the day independently of teachers. Since all children are different in growing and learning patterns, *all of them will handle independence in work habits* in different ways. In classrooms where teachers do not interfere, the use of this freedom is clearly visible during the half hour.

During the same half hour, teachers gather 3 or 4 students at a time to hear the vocabulary homework. This homework is a project in which children decide how much to study at home and/or whether or not to even bring the lesson to school on the next day. What is not free is the meeting with the teacher daily. Students grow in courage and willingness to cooperate as they daily experience a pleasurable meeting with teachers regardless of their own decisions about studying the night before. Now teachers can clearly see *who loves learning, who loves to study, who can be responsible for one's own learning, how children accept each other at the table while waiting* while facing the teacher with the lesson. They *even learn which children are emotionally able to handle the consequences of their decisions to study or not to study!*

Each essential WW activity of the day contains similar types of opportunities for teachers to know daily how *all the children* are learning and how they are progressing in the *process of becoming a person*. Sometimes problems come in the form of unacceptable behavior that hurts the child and others. Remember problems are only clues.

WHAT DO WE DO ABOUT PROBLEMS?

Any child who is consistently showing problematic behavior is automatically considered a Strategy C Learner in WW. A Strategy C Learner is a child who requires speedy human development because human weaknesses of one kind or another stand in the way of the child's learning and growing, accompanied with emotional health. The Strategy C Learning Group is composed of children of every level of knowledge and of every level of mental ability. Knowledge and intelligence do not figure in the policy for placement. All of WW's learning groups call for like personalities with like needs to learn and to work together. Children are in these groups only during the time of the teaching of reading. Throughout the rest of the day *all the children live together in the same workshop*. They choose to work alone or with a partner or with a group of their own selection.

The author's theory is that the kind of behavior human beings express in their daily lives is highly related to the growth point where individuals are in the process of growing and learning. Since *human* development happens as people come to live on higher levels of consciousness in whatever they are doing, saying, or thinking, WW has one kind of learning group designed *by prescription* to daily nourish its members by intense mental involvement. WW's *philosophy* and *psychology* enrich the nourishment because they have power to give the members *feelings* of importance and of *intellectual safety*. As soon as behavior changes indicate a great increase of human development has happened, children are moved to strategies wherein content is moved more speedily. There is a strategy that fits the needs of every child. That is WW's kind of individualization.

As children move along in human development *problems of a disciplinary nature* lessen and can even be removed altogether. There will always be clues, "problems" related to a child's new growth as a learner. It becomes the challenge of the teachers to find ways to satisfy new growth needs in learning; therefore this kind of problem always turns into *process* as a way to solve each problem as it comes along. Learning then becomes exciting for both learners and teachers.

The author has letters from teachers who look forward to each new day because something exciting and fascinating happens every day when learning and growing are the major goals in the environment. Principals have told the author that WW makes good teachers and enhances teachers who have always been good teachers.

Since the workshop tasks in WW are created for the *sole purpose* of social, mental, and personal development, it is not wise for teachers or parents to think "gifted" children need different kinds of jobs. Experience has shown that *all children need human powers, skills, and healthy attitudes towards living and learning.* Gifted children are human beings who have *a right to move towards full human development.* Frequently, gifted children get much knowledge early in their education: this ability to learn knowledge does not automatically nourish human powers, skills and attitudes. Therefore, gifted children need jobs that satisfy human nature in the doing of them, the managing of them, and the finishing of them. Special workshops can be used to challenge students in more difficult subject matter *if the challenges are needed*; but the special workshops do not replace the general workshop. *All children,* by *nature, need the same nourishment for personal, mental, and social growth.* The word "mental" in WW means "level of consciousness." As mental growth moves forward, the degree of consciousness increases. The author has seen many children who were very good students of subject matter be stopped in progressing in human development; the signs of halted growth were usually "cruelty" to self and peers, and other kinds of behavior that made for unpleasant human relationships within the group.

If children are forced to do the tasks the teacher's way, *there*

will be disciplinary problems and sometimes emotional problems.
It hurts a child psychologically if he/she is forced to live lives of
other people on a daily basis rather than living one's own life,
with all its weaknesses and imperfections. At least, fifty years of
experience in teaching and observing children make the author
assume as much. She has seen much unnecessary suffering because of children feeling the pressure of having to appear as if
they were someone else.

Creative ability of "gifted" children should satisfy them in
the *way* they create their arrangements for work and finishing
jobs. There are many free choice activities in the workshop also.

Some Reasons Why Children May Not Learn in School:
WW theory teaches that *all children can learn well in school.*
If they do not, it is because of a lack of some human power,
human skill, or positive attitude towards self and work. Examples:

> courage to move by one's own initiative—not there! wil-
> ingness to risk right or wrong answers in order to learn—
> not there!
> *getting angry when one makes mistakes* (often a weakness in
> the genius and "gifted" children);
> lack of responsibility; and
> lack of love for work and/or learning.

What can be done to remove these weaknesses? All
teaching-learning procedures of stragegy group sessions are of a
nature to bring about many verbal interpersonal relationships between teachers and students. WW's "cushioning" tactics help
children to acquire willingness to make mistakes while learning
and the common sense to accept the mistakes as part of human
existence·with all its limitations. People of all age levels must
submit to being as willing to be wrong as to being right while
they are in the process of learning anything. Adults make this
condition happen sooner if they can drop false values that right
answers are better than wrong answers *for moving human growth*
and that children are worth what they know.

In WW classrooms parents are always welcome as visitors, as

emotional support to their children or to others, and to share their talents should they have any special kind. Problems can be reduced in classrooms if parents could take time to come to school to take the "better" readers out of the room to give them opportunities to read orally, by turn. There is no time in WW's strategy plans for this kind of luxury. I have seen children stay with a parent more than an hour at a time, reading one story after another just for fun.

Positive attitudes in adults and children for learning and living lessen so-called serious problems. Children with opportunities to deepen their feelings of self worth, by the same process, increase their powers *to see, to hear, to read, and to talk.* The more human power children gain, the greater is the probability that they will love to work and to learn.

The powers gained in school have to last a lifetime in order to enable people to meet life's events with willingness to face whatever situations come along and to enable people to continue to live in security.

Feelings in chi'dren are positive and negative. Their moods change frequently. Usually the kind of feelings depends upon what just happened at home or at school or in schoolyard!

It's the negative feelings that adults have to worry about. These can be temporary or can become permanent although sometimes remaining in the subconscious. Adults should desire that the feelings be only temporary. They get their desire *if the activities they direct get children involved in living now in what they are doing.*

If someone makes a lot about the negative feelings and prolongs them in the child's awareness life, these negative feelings can become a real psychological problem for the children.

The length of time the feelings exist in the child's consciousness determines if the feelings become part of the child's personality. *Hence, a long verbal discussion with the child about the feelings deepens the "negativeness" quality in the experience and so nourishes permanency of the suffering* in the child.

It is healthier for the child's emotional development if the problems are not met "head-on" as if they are "bad" things in the mind of child. Hence the importance of teachers and parents to keep children aware of their pleasant experiences, the "good" they do, and the powers they have to handle whatever they are doing.

Talking to children about what appear as big problems or even little ones can also deepen in them a build-up of guilt, real or imaginary.

Teachers and parents must learn how to wait for growth patiently. They can do something while they wait. They get children involved in activities that "shake their brains" to hasten human powers that satisfy living for the children. The activities must call for children to make decisions of some kind or to risk a right or wrong answer.

There are times when principals are asked to help solve the "problems." They use the same suggestions as given above. A child's behavior comes out of his/her present value system. Punishment or scoldings do not advance human growth. Value systems out of which comes acceptable human behavior only change upwards when children reach growth points in human development that are the right condition for giving birth to new values and ideals. Interpersonal relationships that stimulate spontaneous talking on part of child *move human growth*.

This author believes that emotional development follows along with mental development in human beings. Interpersonal relationships are rich nourishment for mental development when they take place on an "intellectual plane" and in situations wherein participants are dead-sure they are safe from humiliations and/or *ridicule*. The *introduction* of this book defines "intellectual plane." The example that follows illustrates a conversation happening on an "intellectual plane."

Johnnie had been disrupting the classroom climate. Her

teacher wanted the principal to talk to her or to do something to take care of this unacceptable behavior.

If the principal's school were a WW school, this is what would happen:

> The principal greets the child with a warm smile and with respectful words. Then *without any reference to child's unsocial behavior,* the principal asks, "Johnnie, you can tell me the difference between a circle and a square, can't you?" Principal waits for *response* with a look of trust.
>
> Then when any answer is given, the principal respects it in some way. Congratulations for the courage it took is one way to make child feel important as a person.
>
> Then principal points to a table and asks, "What about that table, Johnnie, does it make you think of a circle that is round or of a square that is not round?"
>
> Principal allows child to answer the way she wants to, but each new question or remark to child's every response leads child on and on to make decisions—express opinions, and to feel important in interrelating with an adult on same intellectual level, if only in feelings for the time being.

At some point during this conversation, the child will probably suggest that she return to her room. The principal capitalizes on sign of an inner drive in operation and without any reference to "behavior" child returns to classrooms with self respect preserved and enhanced.

WW* *belief* on behavior of
the *growing child:*

Where any child is now in learning and behavior depends upon where his/her growth point is on the scale of human de-

---

*Unacceptable kinds of behavior in school *are not crimes* for which children should be punished. They are clues that cry out for the persons involved, *"help me to get more humanbeingness."*

velopment when the scale is thought of as a process that covers a person's life span—and any growth point on that line is a sign of a percentage of growth on the way to *full human development*.

When the percentage point comes between 50% and 75% and 100%, it is possible that behavior of children gets to be more in harmony with human dignity. The percentage point depends entirely upon the awareness level of one's consciousness of being a person who can learn and think.

Help for Adults:
If a child sulks at first or remains silent: When any adult tries this *way*, smile and do not try until you pause or look warmly at child—one minute later. You may have to wait for another opportunity or another day.

Any negative communication between adults and children weakens *inner drive*, and, if this experience happens daily, inner drive can reach a very low level of being. Any positive communication or sign, such as smiling, strengthens inner drive and nourishes the five basic dispositions people need if they are to reach human development to their fullest potential!

Chapter Six

PLACE OF LEARNING: NON-THREATENING

Why Is a Non-Threatening Place Needed for Learning and Growing Towards Peace at an Early Age?

We have seen in the preceding chapters that a healthy, positive self-concept is essential to the health of a person's *inner drive*. Inner drive is the human being's natural motivational source.

Human beings have within them a strong tendency to fight fiercely to protect their unique possessions of intelligence and worth as persons. If a place insults either of these possessions, it is threatening.

The home is non-threatening if parents allow their children to live without fear of being degraded. It is non-threatening if parents impress their children with all that they do and say that is "good" and keep secret what they see their children do and say that looks "bad" to them right now.

On another day parents can reteach what they think their children should know; that is, what the children didn't know—but they kept that fact a secret at the time they saw the behavior. Reteaching is better than punishment or scoldings or public correction for leading children to deep feelings of their own worth. When parents do the reteaching, no mention can be made about their seeing something "wrong" that other day!

If the word "stupid" is used in the home, the home is

39

threatening. When a place becomes a "testing atmosphere," fear takes over and hurts people. In a non-threatening place, students are dead-sure the adults will not yell at them; they are certain they will be allowed to do their work or play *their way*.

The same things can be said again for the classroom. However, WW does have a safeguard to save security for the students in the classroom. The room is completely child-oriented. The children know clearly the physical organization of the classroom. This clear-cut vision of order and the clear-cut conviction of mastery over the environment in the room make the place non-threatening.

The child thrives on this kind of an environment.

Chapter Seven

PARENTS—TEACHERS: NON-THREATENING

Health of children depends upon adult behavior and attitudes towards them in their growing and learning patterns. It is not meant here to place blame upon adults for children not liking school or not wanting to work in school. Whatever we adults do to children to turn them away from learning is probably done unconsciously because parents and teachers usually love their children.

It is the process of education that is all important!

Adult behavior makes or breaks the power of the learning process to nourish child development.

Attitudes and beliefs of adults about growing children are extremely important as these relate to living and growing at home and in classrooms. Here are some of them:

All children can learn better "with their minds" than they are now doing. I say "with the mind" to make sure the reader will understand I do not mean "learning to sweep the floor" or "learning how to wash the chalkboards."

During the process of growth children show kinds of behavior that adults do not like to see; but they must submit to a willingness to accept these sights with respect and silently wait for growth to move child ahead.

An environment of movement and talking is hard for teachers to allow because this behavior is likely to make other people think there is something "wrong" with them; but growing children need an environment that is deliberately planned to allow them to reveal their true selves. Adults must believe that *children are important enough for them to risk a temporary loss of reputation in order to provide rich nourishment for child development.*

Teachers can keep the talking and movement down by "nagging" but this way stirs up hatred, bitterness, and even cruelty in some students. Children who are victims of nagging get meaner every day. The children may even be forced, if adult nagging continues, to become cruel to others in order to gain opportunities that human beings must have for a "bigness" of person to compensate for the loss of human dignity nourished daily.

What can adults do to help children like this? First, they must stop nagging. Secondly, if the nagging adult is a parent, teachers must work more speedily to nourish the condition of *"intellectual safety"* in the child as soon as possible. *Why?* If a child is deeply convinced of his/her worth as a person, the negative condition in the home can be handled by him/her without loss of emotional balance . . . even if the nagging continues there!

If the nagging adult is the teacher, parents must work speedily to nourish the five basic dispositions at home—which lead to child gaining *"intellectual safety"* faster and so fortifies child to overcome the negative influence in the classroom.

Principle for parents and teachers: Activities used are more powerful if they are always performed on an intellectual plane—forcing children spontaneously to make decisions and choices.

Principle: In the activities, allow a given amount of time for child to take to make a decision or risk. *No one has the right or the knowledge to make a final judgment that any person cannot learn well.* It may look as if the person cannot learn, but no one knows all the reasons why many children do not let us know what they know.

As long as a parent or teacher treats a child who seems to be a "slower learner" with disgust and rejection *even if they do it against their will*, that child suffers tragically in his/her early childhood development.

Punishment is an obstacle that holds back the growth points and prevents children from "growing into" new value systems. Anytime human dignity is insulted, children become mean and bitter towards life and people. They may even rebel openly against authority.

An interesting observation about the WW system of education is that of seeing *mutual respect* come into the environment as soon as children become aware of each one's differences in their humanbeingness.

However, it is not enough to teach children about individual differences. Children must have their belief confirmed by the way they see their parents and teachers give all children equal respect and consideration.

WW's organization of systems and "things" helps teachers to give equal respect to all children. The *instant plans and materials* help teachers to relax, and have security; their emotional health influences the development of the total person in a pleasurable climate.

Chapter Eight

THINGS: NON-THREATENING

Subject matter is a thing. The thing has to be made non-threatening. Every subject matter is a foreign language and must be treated as such. Before people are asked to learn anything, they have a right to hear, say, and see the words and be exposed to concepts of the subject matter on the level of learning in which the students are forced, by law, to live a year at a time, even if students do not or cannot learn it now. Students have the right to get a start in learning "whatever" by planting seeds (language) of concepts in the subconscious mind for retroactive learning.

It is easier for a human being to take orders from a "thing" than from another human being. The "Workshop Schedule" is the thing in WW that controls what children are doing throughout the day. Then regardless of teacher's expertise or nonexpertise, or personality traits, the environment contains nourishment daily for growing and learning.

> The thing relates to all children equally and all children relate to it in a personal way (another instance of WW's kind of individualization!).

> To enjoy studying any subject matter, the vocabulary and the materials must become familiar to the students long before they know the meaning of the words or understand the concepts.

This familiarity gives students a feeling of having met the content somewhere before they are taught it. Example: A textbook can become a task in the workshop early in the year; it will be easy enough to do so that everyone can succeed in it. The assignment shows a page number daily. Students begin there and the minimum requirement is to turn the next ten pages. What each student does as he/she turns the ten pages is very personal; teachers risk what students do (another instance of WW's individualization). Teachers tell students that this seems to be a ridiculous task; but children are assured that some day they will remember what a help this was to them. The task should remain in schedule all year. Each time a person goes through the book he/she is a different person.

This is an example of what WW means when it says that all children have a right to the power that will help them to succeed.

Mistakes and apparent failure are things that have to be made non-threatening. The policy of daily injecting philosophy into the learning situations nourishes students' acceptance of human existence with all it limitations. *Key injections are:*

Do you have to learn this today? Why not? "We just have to get started today."
Is it OK to make a mistake? Why? "That is one way human beings learn."
If John gets his work done before Sally, does that mean John is smarter than Sally? Why not?
Do you ever have to know everything?
Who are you? Do you have to worry about Hank or Jeff doing their work? Why not? "Molly is Molly and Hank is Hank. They have the right to their own time clocks."
Can I make a mistake? Why? "You're just learning" or "You are just human too."

Paper and pencils are things. They are probably the most important things in the whole process. Children *feel very impor-*

tant using paper and pencils. When children have to beg for these things daily, steal them, or get punished and humiliated for not having any, these children suffer emotionally and probably psychologically because it is impossible for them to feel important if they are hurt before they start.

Children come to school to get responsibility; when these essential tools of learning are left to the responsibility of the children, the risk is too great. They have a right to grow according to their own time clocks. They have a right to get the materials in a way that allows them to keep their dignity and respect.

Phrase cards and math cards are things in the workshop. WW uses things to help clear the minds of students. When a child gets to this task, he/she gets the pack of cards. The child sorts cards into two packs—what I don't know and—what I do know. Then the child assumes the responsibility if he/she has some of this power and tries to find someone who will tell him the words.

People are more important than things

Children are free to refuse to help—claiming they are in the midst of their own thing. Teachers should choose opportunities to observe what goes on in these daily quests for help. Much can be learned about the human skills of their children and especially about their attitudes towards learning and peers.

Another Way

The child gets a pack of cards and a partner. Cards are divided. Each child takes a turn to show the cards to the other. One child holds up a phrase card for five counts. Card is hidden behind the person's back. A volunteer says he/she is willing to risk being right or wrong and so gets a chance at being right. A second or third try is legal in partner study.

The handling of these things in the workshop nourishes *inner order*. Inner order is basic to development of self-discipline. Children may need to role-play "asking for help." We are living in an age in history when "asking for help" is not considered an intelligent kind of behavior. "Someone will think I'm stupid if I ask for help." Injections of WW philosophy lead children to have the courage to ask for help. *Asking for help is honorable behavior.*

"Right answers" are things!

This has been discussed earlier in the book.

"Wrong answers" are things, too. They have a very important place in the learning process. This knowledge is essential in leading children towards *intellectual safety*.

An important goal in WW is to give students "intellectual safety" to the degree that neither a person nor an event, even failure, can take away from them their feeling of worth as human beings who can learn and think.

"Intellectual safety" is an inner state or on-going condition that enables people to cope with change and to hold on to *Peace of mind*.

When things in the environment are non-threatening, students *feel safe*. *Security is* a powerful factor for an effective learning condition and for continued health in *peace of mind*.

Chapter Nine

MARKS AND THEIR RELATIONSHIP
TO GROWING AND LEARNING

Marks are a violation of the *principle of individualization*. There is no criteria for marking growth in learning anything that would fit every person at any moment along the way in getting to know the subject matter.

One does not plant a seed and, then, in a few weeks give it an "F" because it is not fully grown yet. How ridiculous it would be if a plant were graded everytime a person saw it. Ever so often a growing plant is observed. At each marking time, it gets "F" because it doesn't have a blossom yet! Finally the blossom comes forth. "Now, plant, you get 'A'."

The policy of marking a plant while in the process of growing seems funny. However, that is how we treat all our children when they are forced to get marked before they are fully grown.

Marks are lethal instruments which can psychologically and emotionally kill the inner drive of human beings. Thousands and thousands of our people have left our schools after ten years of taking home marks that did not satisfy the children, their parents, and their teachers.

No one can ever know what tragic experiences the children suffered and, perhaps, are still suffering, unless some exceptional event helped the children to gain deep feelings of self-worth. Sometimes members of the family called the child "stupid." It isn't unusual for parents and/or siblings to introduce the family with: "This is the smart one! This is the slow one!"

It is the nature of human beings to be highly vulnerable to insults that sting them intellectually, even consciously. Inner drive is weakened each time this experience happens.

In the process of killing inner drive, some people have recourse to withdrawal behavior and others choose aggressive behavior to fight for intellectual survival.

Marks do not tell anyone anything because teachers who decide them are all different and teachers are highly influenced by their own value systems. If marks are good, the ego of parents and teachers is satisfied. If not good, the ego of the adults is deflated. All is well as long as the good marks are there. Let the good marks stop for whatever reason, and the adults unconsciously feel pain and guilt. The children suffer as victims upon whom all the blame is laid. Because they have been given the false value that they have worth only if they have good marks, there is little they can do to help themselves.

Some educators believe marks are necessary in order to motivate students for learning. If that is true, it might explain the educational problems of today. There would be many students without motivation. Genuine motivation could be everyone's possession if the first thrust of the educational process aimed to develop human skills and powers first in order to make inner drive strong.

About Report Cards
In regard to report cards, there has to be another way for healthy communications between the home and school. The author sees great value in sending home report cards for parents to mark several times a year during the first six months of the school year. The next page shows a sample of a report card for parents.

PARENT SHARING WITH TEACHERS

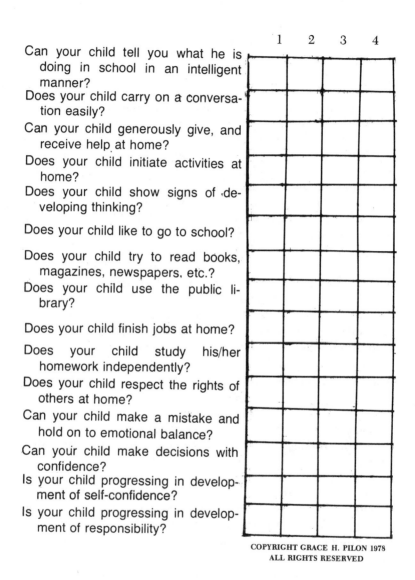

	1	2	3	4
Can your child tell you what he is doing in school in an intelligent manner?				
Does your child carry on a conversation easily?				
Can your child generously give, and receive help at home?				
Does your child initiate activities at home?				
Does your child show signs of developing thinking?				
Does your child like to go to school?				
Does your child try to read books, magazines, newspapers, etc.?				
Does your child use the public library?				
Does your child finish jobs at home?				
Does your child study his/her homework independently?				
Does your child respect the rights of others at home?				
Can your child make a mistake and hold on to emotional balance?				
Can your child make decisions with confidence?				
Is your child progressing in development of self-confidence?				
Is your child progressing in development of responsibility?				

With such a card, the school helps parents to look for the good things their children have going for them. The home helps teachers because the report cards furnish information that helps them to know where the children are in learning and in growing.

How Would Parents Mark the Report Cards?

A 4-point scale is placed after each item. The meaning of the code is as follows:

1. Parents see this behavior consistently.
2. Parents see behavior often.
3. They see the behavior only occasionally.
4. They never see the behavior.

Since the procedures in the strategy groups are geared to nourish the precise human skills or powers that the child has need of, this new kind of communication with parents can be extremely helpful.

A Plea to Parents

What is being said here can only be said to parents who have children in WW classrooms. It takes a few children more than one year to get a very good foundation in the basics and especially in developing their five basic dispositions. *When children start living in WW classroom climate,* few of them need more than one year on any level for growing. Should your child be recommended for that privilege of remaining another year on same WW level of learning please remember—a second year in a WW set-up will always find the child in the strategy A or B sessions the second year. If the child goes on to new level *without* full human growth of previous level, most likely the child will be a Strategy C Learner in every level all the way through school. A Strategy C Learner is not a child with a stigma; but teachers and parents have a right to expect on-going growth in human powers and skills. Sending Strategy C Learners to next grade level without these powers and skills developed to right degree of awareness is a predictable obstacle to human development on next

51

level. The plea is to ask you parents to say—yes—if the teacher suggests that your child needs another year in the same classroom. However, this recommendation is made only for children who can remain in the WW the second year. If the child would continue in same grade but to a different kind of school, I could not predict the same success.

Chapter Ten

THE WORKSHOP WAY®

The name of this book is *Peace of Mind at an Early Age*. This system of human development for education creates the conditions inside the child and outside the child which lead students towards the dead-sure feeling of "intellectual safety," a life-line of security for survival throughout the days of their lives. With that kind of security all children can learn how to read and talk with self-confidence. The system is especially suitable for people who live in a democracy.

Watching children in a kindergarten manage their doings by means of a schedule, a "thing," which they follow independently of their teachers, is an interesting experience. Adults sometimes forget that children like to play "making believe being adults." The WW organization provides them with a perfect setting for this managing of their lives as "adults." Through living the activities in this set-up, children gain true values that relate to their worth. They become convinced, at age 5, that they are persons who can learn and think—and even make mistakes while doing it all. That's *the formula for peace of mind.*

Dr. Daniel P. Heisler, Associate Professor of Bowling Green University, Ohio, has this to say about WW:

> The WW is the most human thing that I have seen in public schools in my 30-years' experience in them. I have seen

children begin to enjoy school, to begin to learn because it is fun to learn. But, best of all, I've seen children begin to believe in themselves.

Yes, WW uses content to change behavior. It does change behavior. The change comes from within and as a bonus children learn more, too.

All children have a right to discover within them the power to think, to learn, and to handle their lives!

If any students come to school unable to learn, teachers provide a way to create the power to learn in them.

The Six Elements of Workshop Way® are:

1. Conditioning the physical environment of the classroom to create a work-life climate for children to live in all day except when they are being taught by teachers.

Core Power: "Workshop Schedule"

Core Power is the "factor" created by the system's use of materials and procedures that causes the nourishment for human development to exist while teachers and students live "learning the content."

2: Conditioning the social environment of the classroom to create many interpersonal relationships throughout the day.

Core Power: *Five Freedoms* and the *Positive Attitudes*, of the teachers towards learning and the learners.

3. A Self-Concept Vocabulary Project to nourish and develop a positive self-concept in each child.

Core Power: *Personal gaze* and *independent handling of whatever happens each morning between teachers and students.*

Opportunity to make a major decision each night on how much to study.

4. Instant Personality-Phonics Activities which contain more nourishment for Personality Development.

Core Power: The system supplies the *"instant"* factor in the plans and materials.
Five activities happen daily to insure children will have nourishment for personality growth.
* communicate with a smile
* feel power for learning something
* feel dead-sure of having learned a lot
* feel learning a little more each day
* have opportunity to risk using knowledge without fear of humiliation

5. Parental involvement to make home-school relations healthy.

Core Power: Parents know they can go into their child's classroom whenever they want.

6. Use of time, content, and strategies to individualize person power.

Core Power:

1) groups based on personalities;
2) The major content of any level of learning is the content used with strategy procedures.

Motivation: Inner Drive
The human basic needs of students that need satisfying in the process are:

a dead-sure feeling of intellectual safety within the person;
a state of inner order in the brain that affords security and a

55

feeling of self-confidence in person;

the ability to create, to organize, and to follow through on ideas regardless of what others think;

doing satisfying work on one's own time and with security in knowing one is not in competition with peers; and

the sense of cooperation the willingness to risk in order to learn.

Dual System

Children live all day in the workshop except when they are taught in groups.

Teachers teach all day in any kind of a structure.

By *"Dual System,"* WW means an educational framework in which children have their responsibility in the system and teachers have their responsibilities in the system. Students start each day by doing the tasks of a workshop independently of their teachers. They are free to go to friends for needs, sharing, and for okaying work once in a while on specific occasions.

Teachers are responsible for *preparing the environment* and for the teaching of the content of whatever the grade level requires in any school system.

Teachers are free to teach any way, at any time, throughout the day. WW calls these ways—*"structures."* There is the structure of the whole class lesson, the group structure to match the needs of students in "where they are" in humanbeingness. There is the one-to-one structure during the first half hour daily.

The flexibility of the WW structure is that when *it is no longer needed*, another structure takes its place in order to allow students to·continue on to higher stages of consciousness in the business of learning and growing.

WW's structure is highly flexible at all times.

All children need speedy movement towards a positive self-concept *early in their educational development.* They cannot wait until they succeed academically for a healthy self-concept. The source of the positive self-concept cannot be a favor that might be here today and gone tomorrow. It must be a factor that is a *truth about human beings* that children become convinced that they have because they become aware of having powers that all persons can have. When the awareness is deep enough, children unconsciously or consciously say to themselves:

"I know I don't have to know everything!"
"I know lots of things!"
"I know I can make a mistake and still be and feel intelligent!"
"I'm not afraid to make a mistake."
"I know I can ask a friend for help and still be intelligent."
"I know what I know from what I don't know."
"I know I can handle things—whatever happens!"
"I know what I'm going right now and I can tell you!"
"I know *you can do all this too!*"

When children believe these things about themselves, *they live continuously in an affective state for learning well.*

This system for education insures that children will have some lessons every day by means of *instant plans and instant materials* in some subject matter. All children see, hear, and say the foundational language of their subject matter. Familiarity with the language raises the probability level that children will learn the subject matter. *The understanding of the language and materials is not required at the time* students are becoming familiar with these elements.

Therefore, all students have equal opportunities for participating and forming a learning condition for future successful learning and understanding.

HOW DOES WW JOIN AFFECTIVE
AND COGNITIVE LEARNING?

A. In its techniques

1) *Personal gaze* makes children *feel important while* they are in the act of handling what they learned.
2) *Opportunity to handle grade level content* before learning it well makes children *feel secure now* because they do not have to know the content and makes them feel important later on because they will know the content.
3) *Familiarity with language*—while discovering they know much of it—homework policy of dotting words known before leaving table if new lesson was received because old lesson was lost.
4) "Cushioning" children to be willing to make mistakes while learning.
5) *Living knowledge daily*—activity in phonics.
6) *Volunteer policy*—Are you willing to be wrong or right? Whole class repeats answer with power.

B. Policies

1) Consistency of teachers to be at homework table the first thing every morning—success does not depend upon knowledge skills.
2) Children take home a letter on the first day of school. One section reads as follows·

Parents, we do not want you to tell or make children study their homework. The purpose of this project is to develop *initiative* in children to ask for help, if they need it or to share the joy of their knowing with parents, if they need support and satisfaction. We only ask you to always say (something like), "Yes. I'll be happy to do that for you."

58

3) Children learn new things in group sessions with peers whose personality traits are compatible. Mutual respect is present; hence, children feel secure while learning.

4) The mid-session count-checks of finished work that all children are capable of finishing regardless of mental ability today—allow students to know and to feel they have worth.

C. Philosophy

1) Children are dead-sure their teachers will not humiliate them while they are learning.

2) Parents and teachers are asked to praise human skills every time they see them. Adults assure students who ask for help with words, "I'm so glad you had enough sense to ask." This makes child feel important.

3) Children are daily cushioned towards development of intellectual safety. Knowledge skills are not praised. Children get to believe that they are worth more than "things."

4) Giving and asking for help are honorable kinds of behavior. Children are free to take the initiative to take care of things that might happen during school hours (honorable behavior). A child's behavior is personal business. Teachers don't talk to them about good or bad behavior.

D. Strategy Session Techniques

1) Strategy A Learners continue to read story every day in presence of teachers. Children read in low tone of voice. Teachers are dead-sure each child is growing in self-confidence. Children become sure they are learning. Students handle their activities independently of teachers. There is daily checking of workbooks which were worked entirely without the teachers. Children

get to believe in themselves. Only right answers are checked in workbooks.

2) Strategy B Learners: Children know for sure the sequence of activities that will happen every day. They are not threatened by what might happen. They know. This knowing makes children feel secure.

The 5-second phrase drill makes everyone *feel* successful and feel important.

Children handle their own study of story daily in presence of teachers. Teachers know they know so children know they know. *Security is felt.*

Scratch Pad Technique exercises minds for mental alertness rather than totally for comprehension. *Awareness of power to think is deepened.*

Fast oral reading makes children feel important. Knowledge of subject matter and potential mental abilities *are not used as criteria for membership* in the three learning strategies. Grouping is by *like personalities.* Students on every level are reading ALL OF THE TIME in reading lessons daily. Blocks of reading time are not used for times to discuss anything—on a teacher-one student manner. *One learns how to read by reading.* Personality Grouping safeguards *human dignity* in all strategy groups.

3) Strategy C Learners: 100% of children will finish a task before reading time is over because of daily check for "finishing."

Finishing leads to child feeling important.

Opportunity daily to be willing to be wrong when challenged to pick up cards they know. Willing involvment nourishes feeling of importance.

Free choice readers—*all* children are reading in low tone of voice—they get to believe they are reading. Awareness of this belief makes one feel important as a PERSON.

All children work at "yes-no" exercises daily in presence of teachers who encourage them to risk answers without looking on back of the "yes-no" card. *All children* participate in a "brain-shaking" activity daily which involves them at a high degree of mental activity.

Evidence exists which shows increased pupil learning and more positive attitudes as a result of the WW system. In many classes using WW across the country, there are frequent days of 100% attendance.

Dr. Maurice Martinez, Jr., Assistant Professor in Education at Hunter College, New York City, has this to say:

The "Workshop Way" system of pedagogy insures success . . . develops within the child a strong self-concept, a comfortable sense of inner direction and self-discipline, an interesting respect of the rights of others, along with rapid progress in reading, arithmetic, and writing skills.

All living creatures need tender loving care;

    BUT

        THAT

          IS

            NOT

              ENOUGH

                FOR

                  HUMAN BEINGS!!!!!

HUMAN BEINGS need:
      TENDER

         INTELLECTUAL

           CARE!!!

They need: NON-THREATENING

         PERSONS

         PLACES

         THINGS

         in their educational
and HOME ENVIRONMENTS!

* * * * * * * * * *

Children *cannot* take their teachers home with them for on-going "tender loving care."
However, they can take their new human growth home which "tender intellectual care" gives them from WITHIN.

* * * * * * * * * *

The five freedoms which children need in a healthy learning climate and which help to create the work-life environment in the classrooms are:

    freedom from fear
    freedom of movement
    freedom of position and location for work
    freedom of conversation while working
    freedom of choice throughout the day

WORKSHOP WAY® BOOKS by Grace H. Pilon

The Workshop Way®, Inc.
7325 Palmetto Street
New Orleans, LA 70125

1. THE WORKSHOP WAY®, a manual for the total program—any grade level
2. PHILOSOPHY and PSYCHOLOGY OF A WW DAY
3. SELF-CONCEPT and READING, the WW (K-4)
4. DAILY LOGS from a WW FIRST GRADE CLASSROOM
5. WW FIRST GRADE HANDBOOK
6. WW PRACTICAL HANDBOOK, for elementary and intermediate teachers
7. INSTANT PERSONALITY—PHONICS ACTIVITIES®—Grade One (lesson plans)
8. MATERIALS CUT-OUT BOOK, for #7 above.
9. INSTANT PERSONALITY—PHONICS ACTIVITIES®—Grade Two (plans)
10. MATERIALS CUT-OUT BOOK, for #9 above
11. INSTANT PERSONALITY—PHONICS ACTIVITIES®—Grade Three (plans)
12. MATERIALS CUT-OUT BOOK, for #11 above
13. ARITHMETIC THE WW—Grade One (lesson plans that can be used with any publisher's textbooks)
14. WORKSHOP WAY® MATH—Book Two (plans go with any textbooks—plans adaptable to content of higher levels of learning)
15. "THINKERS" K-1, 147 "Thinkers," as described in THE WORKSHOP WAY® and in SELF-CONCEPT and READING THE WW ("Thinkers" that can be made easily by teachers are not included)
16. INSTANT PERSONALITY ACTIVITIES for KINDERGARTEN, and other groups of children in Special Education and in pre-school gifted education
17. MATERIALS CUT-OUT BOOK, for #16 above
18. WW KINDERGARTEN HANDBOOK

19. THE "WORKSHOP SCHEDULE"—220 task signs and description of tasks—also an eleven-page discussion on the workshop for all grades, K-8

INFORMATION FOR TEACHER NEEDS AT DIFFERENT LEVELS OF LEARNING

Kindergarten: Numbers 3, 15, 16, 17, 18

First Grade: Numbers 1, 3, 5, 7, 8, 13, 15 Helpful, not essential: 2, 4

Second Grade: Numbers 1, 3, 6, 9, 10, 14 Helpful, not essential: 2

Third Grade: Numbers 1, 3, 6, 11, 12 Helpful, not essential: 2, 14

Fourth Grade: Numbers 1, 3, 6, (if phonics/English are needed, Grade 3 plans are suitable) 2, 14

5th through 8th grades: 1, 2, 6, 14

High School: 1, 14 (organizational framework of philosophy and psychology for the teaching of any subject matter, even foreign languages